The Little Book of

By

JM Werrett

Introduction

Crystals

Herbs & Spices

Spells

Tarot

Dreams

Superstitions

I am so excited to be writing this! It feels a little naughty because I have always felt the need to hide who I am. Not that I have hidden it, but I have learned that most people think my beliefs are nonsense and so I keep them to myself unless I feel the need to debate.

So what do I believe? Well I believe in a universal energy or soul that runs through all things. The energy will be different within each of us as we are all different parts of the whole but if we want to attract certain things into our lives then we need to change our energy field. Our energy acts like a magnet attracting situations, people and things based on the energy we project. For most of us it can be difficult keeping that energy positive due to illness or the subconscious and so when we want to attract certain things into our lives we need to make an extra effort. The problem is that when our own energy gets blocked in some way it can make us ill and disconnect us from the whole. Energy blocks can be cleared through meditation, natural therapies and crystals.

Colours, crystals, plants and herbs all give off vibrations that will help you to make your message to the universe stronger so use them.

So throughout the book I will give you spells or as I prefer to think of them, energy work, and tips for doing this but always remember to use your intuition. To conduct a spell and to consciously draw a certain energy into your life is one and the same thing!

Crystals

Larimar

Larimar is said to give you a direct line to the universal life source. It's related to the element of water and is said to embody the power and mystery of the seas. As this is a healing stone Larimar is said to help to heal you of past hurts and promote the balance you need to attract your soul mate.

Rose Quartz

Rose quartz helps with all kinds of love. It opens the heart chakra and helps to promote a loving energy. As well as helping to attract love this stone will also help to strengthen existing love. It is probably always a good idea to use this with a love spell or to attract love to a home.

Rhodochrosite

This stone will help you to love yourself and to attract unconditional love into your life.

Citrine

Citrine is a beautiful golden colour stone that will not only attract prosperity but will also aid you in visualising what you desire. If you are going to use it in meditation or wear it to attract abundance it should be kept near your solar plexus (around the area of your belly button).

Pyrite

Pyrite, also known as 'fool's gold' is an excellent talisman for good luck. It protects you both spiritually and physically and will help you to achieve your goals with confidence.

Peridot

Is a great stone for attracting money. Keep it in your purse with a piece of citrine for best results.

Amazonite

Amazonite will create a feeling of love inside of you. It will allow you to see your true self and to love yourself without judgement. It will give you courage and clarity and help you with psychic work.

Azurite

Azurite will help you to let go of the negative self talk and sneaky little thoughts of the past that creep into your mind and stop you from attracting what you want into your life. By letting go of all that holds you back you will see your future more clearly. It will also help you to connect with the spirit world.

Unakite

Unakite is a very interesting stone as it helps uncover truth. If you feel that your partner is lying to you give them a piece of unakite and await the results. Wear it when performing a spell to give you confidence and increase your intention.

Amber

Amber has been used by witches for many years and is sacred to the Goddess Freya. It is a powerful stone of protection and helps to attract passion and increase fertility. You can also use this stone if you need to feel strong.

Chiastolite

The fairy cross. Use this stone to attract the fairy folk and ask for their help in all things magical.

Tiger eye

Tiger eye is a good stone for protection and for keeping away bad dreams. It is very powerful when used for attracting love or passion and will increase your confidence.

Sugilite

A great stone to use for all things magical and it is often said that when this stone is used by those with pure intentions it can change the world. This stone will help you to see the workings of the law of attraction and to follow your dreams.

Smokey quartz

Smokey quartz will help you to access other realms of existence and communicate with other energy beings. It can enhance spiritual growth and is great for scrying.

Red jasper

Use this stone for spells involving passion or protection. It can help keep away nightmares and protect you from harm. It is often used to contact demonic energies and can help you to access demonic knowledge.

Phenacite

This stone is said to awaken and strengthen the spirit within. It will help you to understand your true abilities and to use them for a better life.

Feldspar

Keep some in a pouch with a silver coin. This stone will help you to hear spirit.

Iolite

Iolite is a great stone for spell work. It will enhance all types of energy and increase your psychic ability. It will improve your visualisation skills and help you to focus and grow. It will increase the magic in your life.

Jacinth

This stone will make you very difficult to resist! It will increase your magnetism and protect you from illness. It will also help you to get your own way with others. When sending an important letter place a piece of this on it for 3 hours before you send it!

Golden quartz

I have one of these. When I am feeling in need of guidance I take one to bed and my dreams are vivid with clear messages. Known as the master healer this is a great stone for use with energy healing, meditation and spiritual work. It is said to raise your vibration and fill you with the universal energy.

Herbs, flowers and spices

Apple blossoms

The blossoms from an apple tree are said to be very powerful. Place them in your bath, carry them with you and use them in spells to attract admirers.

Basil

Basil has been used in magic for a long time and legend has it that it was once used to cure madness and drank by witches before they went flying on broomsticks! Basil has many magical properties and can be used to attract money, happiness or love. You can keep a basil plant in your house, place some by your bed, carry some in your pocket or use it in spells.

Bay leaves

Bay leaves will help you to attract your soul mate! Keep them near your bed or in your pocket and use them in spells.

Jasmine

Jasmine will attract love and money and is said to give you really vivid dreams that will help you to delve into your subconscious! It is also an aphrodisiac so good for attracting passion. I love to burn jasmine oil around the home as it smells gorgeous but you can buy a plant or use the oil around the home, in your bath and a must for spells!

Allspice

A very good spice for attracting money and success. Keep some in a pouch in your purse or sprinkle in the four corners of your home.

Cinnamon

Cinnamon is excellent if you want to attract large amounts of money quickly. It also attracts luck, love and health.

Ginger

Ginger is another good spice for attracting wealth and is also good for passion.

Mint

Now according to ancient wisdom rubbing mint into the money in your purse will attract more of it. Keep some mint in your wallet or purse to attract money.

Acorn

An acorn is a very powerful talisman and should be kept on your person for luck, wisdom and protection. It is also said to keep your appearance young and beautiful.

Almond

Use almond for wisdom, prosperity and to invoke the higher powers. Wear it to attract abundance.

Bergamot

Bergamot will attract money and protect you physically, keeping you healthy of body and mind. It is very powerful for attracting success and if you use during spell work it will increase the power.

Blackberry

Sacred to the Goddess Brigit blackberry will provide a protective energy and to attract prosperity and healing.

Blueberry

Toss a little blueberry into the path of an enemy to cause them confusion and strife!

Carnation

A lovely magical flower. Use them in your bath or spells for luck, money and protection. They will also help to increase your magical strength.

Willow

Willow is great for moon magic and for drawing love into your life. It is considered a sacred wish tree and you should wear it if you face the death of a loved one. Keep some in the home for protection. I have a branch tangled in a white wicker love heart in my bedroom window!

Witch hazel

Carry some to help ease the pain of losing a loved one.

Tobacco

Mix it with salt and burn it with a black candle to gain victory in legal matters!

Thyme

Add some to your bath to ensure a constant flow of money. You should also bath in it before performing magic as it will clear your energy field and allow you to project the desired intent.

Tea

Burn tea leaves to attract riches.

Pomegranate

It is said that if you eat a pomegranate whilst visualising a wish your wish will come true.

Orange

Orange will attract abundance and a happy marriage. It is said that if you concentrate on a yes/no question you want answered while eating an orange it will give you the answer through the seeds. An odd number of seeds means yes and an even number means no. Add it to your bath for beauty and use for love spells.

Onion

Onions can be used for prosperity and abundance. If you cut an onion in half and place in the corners of a room they will absorb illness. Bury the onion halves in the morning.

Ivy

Ivy will bring love and protection. If you hang it in the home it will keep away unwanted guests and keep the energy positive.

Honeysuckle

Honeysuckle attracts prosperity and success. It will attract confidence and strengthen your intuitive power. Carry some in a pouch to attract money and rub a little into your forehead for psychic ability.

Oak

The oak is a very sacred tree and great to use for making a wand. It can be used for fertility, positivity and to strengthen the family. Carry some for wisdom and strength.

Nutmeg

Nutmeg will attract money, prosperity and good luck. Carry it as a talisman or use it to anoint your green candle for money magic.

Dandelion root

Make the root into a tea to open gateways to other realms. Use it for wish magic and calling spirits and bury it outside your home to the north to attract luck.

Spells

Spells work on an energy level. The law of attraction works with our intent to draw the desired outcome into our lives. You should be aware that the subconscious can often keep these things out of our energy field. Money attracts money, love attracts love so in order for your spell to work you should try to always be in the mindset of abundance. Always be grateful for everything and everyone you have in your life. Every day thank the universe for giving you a roof over your head, money in your bank, food in the cupboard and the people in your life. This is the most important part.

Before you cast any spell remember that your intention should always be positive! If it isn't you risk the negative energy coming back three fold. The best time to do a spell is around the New Moon. The energy of the New Moon

will work with you in the creation and manifestation of your desire.

You should also have something there to represent the elements of earth, air fire and water (stones, candles, herbs, water or incense).

Before I do a spell I like to draw a circle with my finger that I can work within. This will surround me with light, protective energy. Then I stand in my circle and visualise the universal energy rising through me like a spiral of light.

When it reaches my hands I draw a pentacle in the air while saying:

I know by the power of air

By the power of water I dare

By fire I wield my will

By earth I am silent still

And in my heart and height I tread my road aright, blessed be.

Another little chant which I love can be said to put your intent into an object like a candle or wand.

Thine eyes my eyes

Thy hand my hand

All of thee caught and confused with me

Days

Each day of the week corresponds to a different planet and so will help you to direct your energy.

Sunday
Sunday is the day associated with the sun and on this day you should conduct spells related to business, career success, friendship and health.

Monday
Ruled by the Moon, use this day to work on issues of fertility, home and psychic ability.

Tuesday
Ruled by Mars, this is day is best used for all things masculine like conflict, competition, protection.

Wednesday
Ruled by Mercury, this is the best day for anything related to inspiration, communication and learning.

Thursday
Ruled by Jupiter, use this day for anything related to money, prosperity and luck.

Friday
Ruled by Venus, use this day for anything related to love and matters of the heart.

Saturday
Ruled by Saturn, use this day for anything related to death, past lives, spirit world.

Spells to attract love

Venus is the associated planet for love and the day to communicate with Venus is Friday. Colours are red or pink.

A spell to reunite with a lost love

Day: Friday

Time: 9pm

What you need: 1 red or pink candle, jasmine or rose oil, one of the above crystals.

The most important thing with any spell is your intent. Visualise what you want. If you have a photograph use that too. Carve the name of your lost love into the candle while visualising your reunion. Try to feel the emotions you would feel, try to feel the love that you have for him/her. When you have finished carving the name rub the oil over the candle. As you light the candle and put it in a safe place to burn say the following words:

Universal energy, bring my lost love back to me,

As candle burns so mote it be

Universal energy, bring my lost love back to me

As candle burns so mote it be

Universal energy bring my lost love back to me

As candle burns so mote it be

Allow your candle to burn until it goes out naturally placing the crystal and any other objects you have around it. As I said earlier make sure it's in a safe place and not near any curtains or anything else that could catch fire.

A spell to bring back a lost love

Day: Friday

Time: 9pm

What you need: Red candle to place in the south, green candle for the north, yellow candle for the east, blue candle for the west, a pink candle for your lost love, crystal that we mentioned earlier, jade or rose oil.

After drawing up the energy as I mentioned earlier place the coloured candles in their corresponding direction in your circle if you have made one. Holding the pink candle:

I call upon you gatekeepers of the watchtowers of the south and I ask that you guide my wish

I call upon you gatekeepers of the watchtowers of the north and I ask that you guide my wish

I call upon you gatekeepers of the watchtowers of the east and I ask that you guide my wish

I call upon you gatekeepers of the watchtowers of the west and I ask that you guide my wish

I call to venus burning bright, that she may guide my love tonight

Guide him safe, guide him strong, guide him to me where he belongs

And if it harms none so mote it be.

Let the candles burn out naturally, making sure they are in a safe place!

Spell to attract love

Day: Friday

Time: 9pm

What you need: A pink or red ribbon, jasmine or rose oil

Rub the oil into your hands and pull the ribbon through, covering it in the oil as you are visualising love in your life. Then you will tie 3 knots saying:

I tie knot one my love shall come

I tie knot two to make it true

As I tie three so mote it be!

Keep the ribbon near your bed or close to you.

Spell to attract love

Day: Any

Time: Any

What you need: Mint, Lavender, Rose, Rosemary, Thyme, Vanilla, a piece of paper describing the person that you desire, pink candle.

Take as many of the above plants as you can find and chop them, mix them together. Put them in a fire proof bowl along with your paper that describes the person you want in your life. With your pink candle light the paper while saying:

By power of flame and words of soul

My wish I burn within this bowl

Send my heart's desire to me

By the power of three so mote it be!

When the paper has burnt scoop the ashes along with the plants/herbs into your pouch and carry them with you.

Marriage spell

When: Full moon

What time: 9pm

What you need: A white dish, a white rose, a silver ring, rosemary, thyme and cardamom

The day before you do the spell put the herbs and the ring in the bowl. On the following night hold the ring up to the moon and look at the moon through ring as you say:

Bring to me my heart's desire

My love for him will never die

By the light of this full moon

Bring me marriage soon, soon, soon!

Then hold the rose up so that it covers the moon from your view and repeat the verse. When you have done that place the ring over the stem of the rose and place it in the dish saying the verse one more time. Leave your spell in the window and it should show results by the next full moon.

Spells to attract money and prosperity

Jupiter is the planet for money and the day associated with Jupiter is Thursday. Colours are green or gold.

Spell to attract money

Day: Any

Time: Any

What you need: Essential oils myrrh or patchouli will work well, green candle

Anoint your candle with your oil while visualising yourself surrounded by a green aura. Money is being pulled into your aura as if it's a strong money magnet. Hold this thought for around 30 seconds before lighting the candle and saying:

Money, money come to me

Gift me with prosperity

Give me all that I can see

And times by three so mote it be!

Say the verse three times and leave the candle in a safe place to burn down.

Spell to attract money

Day: During a full moon

Time: 9pm

What you need: A dish preferably silver, a silver coin and a green candle.

During the full moon, in view of the full moon place the coin the in the dish of water and repeatedly run your hands through the water visualising your gathering of the moons silver beams and say:

Lady, lady of the moon

Bring to me your riches soon

Bring to me silver and gold

And far more than my purse can hold

Repeat this three times under the light of the moon and pour the water onto the earth. Keep the coin with you or in your bedroom window.

A spell for money

Day: Any

Time: Any

What you need: Lavender, a little pouch, 7 different types of money

Put your money (a penny, 10p, 50p, £1 etc) in the pouch and sprinkle with the lavender. Carry the money with you for 7 days and it should be returned multiplied by 7.

Money spell

Day: Thursday

Time: 9pm

What you need: A few strands of your own long hair or a few green threads

Roll the hair back and forth in your hands to make it one thick thread and begin to tie 9 knots in it while saying:

Lord and lady send to me

Lots of money, times by three

Let it come innocently

And harm to none so mote it be

Say the verse three times while visualising yourself with lots of money. After the knots have been tied burn the hair and throw the ashes to the wind thanking the universe for hearing your wish.

A money spell

Day: Thursday

Time: 9pm

What you need: Green candle, needle or pin, an oil or herb to anoint candle (basil would work well, or myrrh).

Using the pin write the amount of money you need on the candle while visualising your gain. Anoint the candle with your oil and light it. Let it burn out naturally.

With money spells always ensure to give something back. Donate to charity or give to someone who needs it.

Spells for protection

This is a lovely little spell for protection. Take some clay and make a dragon. When you have made him prick your finger and rub the blood over the dragon's heart. Give him a name and call it three times and say the following three times:

As I will it come to life

Protect me from all kinds of strife

When in need I'll call your name

Times three, so mote it be!

You will feel the life come into your dragon at some point. Call his name three times when you need him.

Day: Tuesday

Time: 9pm

What you need: Yellow or white candle.

Light your candle and visualise it filling your home with protective energy whilst placing it in your window sill and saying the following three times:

Charge this candle by my will

The white one on my window sill

With power of sun and moon and me

Protecting me, so mote it be

Or if you prefer you could make your own verse or say:

Mother moon please hear my plea

Through candle fire please protect me

Through night and day keep me from harm

As candle burns please seal my charm

A protection spell for quick temporary protection

Visualise yourself or the object in need of protection surrounded by a beautiful pale blue light. As you do so repeat the words:

Goddess with your light so bright

Protect (name) with all your might

Keep it safe from harm or deed

Surround (name) with your golden seed

So mote it be

Spell to protect you throughout the day

Stand upright with your eyes closed visualising a beautiful blue energy field all around you. Feel the tingling of the light energy all around your body, move your hands slowly feeling them brush through the energy. As you do so say these words three times:

Universal energy surround me through this day

Protect from negativity and harm in every way

The power of blue stay with me throughout my time of need

Safe and warm, protected from all outside of me

Spell to protect your home

Day: Any

Time: Any

What you need: Jar or bottle, masonry nails or holly leaves, frankincense.

Ok so you anoint your jar with frankincense or any other oil that can be used for protection. Then you fill it with nails or holly leaves and as you do say the following three times:

Sunday, Monday, Mars and Sun

This jar is made for protection

Guard my home both day and night

Protect my home with all your might

Place the jar or bottle in a safe place where it won't be disturbed preferably inside a wall or close to a wall.

These spells are just guides. When you understand that colours, fragrances, plants and stones all carry a certain energy you can make your own spells. The words can be written by yourself as an offering to the higher realms. Visualise and hold the intention whilst doing your spells. It takes around 20 seconds for a thought or vibration to attract energy from the universe.

So make your own spells and enjoy! Be sure to keep a little diary so that you can record the results.

The Tarot Cards

The tarot cards are like a mysterious and magical best friend. They are always there to guide and speak the truth as long as you pose a clear question. Readings should be done based on your intuition, use as many as you think you should and label them as you think best.

The tarot represents a journey of self discovery. Each card is an archetype of a part of our psyche. When you are reading the cards for someone you should do the reading based on what the cards mean to you.

The Fool

I won't focus too much on the description of the pictures of the cards because each deck will differ in the images so because of that we will discuss meaning.

Do you wish to start a new life? A new phase or project? The fool tells us of new beginnings and tells us that in order to progress we may have to take calculated risks. You have all that you need to start afresh. Don't be afraid but be sure to evaluate all of your options first so that you don't end up looking foolish!

The Magician

The magician is highlighting your skills or ability to manifest change. Change may be needed and in order to create that you should first start with changing your perception. You have many tools available to move forward so choose carefully the right one for your purpose. One small change can be a catalyst to set bigger changes in motion.

The magician tells you that you do have the power but with great power comes great responsibility! Can you handle the consequences?

The High Priestess

The high priestess is calling you to study the wisdom within. She also tells you that everything is as it should be so sometimes the only choice you have is to let things be. Accept that things are the way they are and let this particular situation be. Look within and learn to understand and accept yourself, until you do that you will continue to attract problems outside of you.

Our soul has a purpose and sometimes chooses to live a challenging life here on earth because it stimulates growth within. Negativity as well as positivity in our lives offer great gifts.

The knowledge that you seek is inside of you. It always was. Sometimes you just need to quiet the mind and let the world float away as you take an inner journey. Meditate and you will find the answers.

The Empress

Whenever I have drawn this card it has been to tell me that I am pregnant. This card points to feminine qualities, fertility, pregnancy, empathy and wisdom. You may be called upon to offer guidance and things will be going well for you career wise. You are inspirational and passionate, allow your intuition to guide you. This is a time for abundance.

You may find yourself gaining more attention from men and women and if single this could be a good time for you to find a deep love.

The Emperor

I remember one reading I did where this card was the first to be drawn. For some reason I asked the lady if an older had passed away, someone who had unfinished business with her. Suddenly the atmosphere of the room changed and as her eyes filled with tears she told me it was her father. The reading turned out to be a long message from her deceased father who was trying to put things right for her peace of mind.

The Emperor is symbolic of authority, of masculinity. The emperor is stating that you have the power to take your life in any direction you wish. You are the master of your destiny. You deserve to be respected but you need to find respect for yourself to allow that. Don't allow other people's influence to affect your life decisions and emotions. Take charge.

The Hierophant

This card represents formal learning. He interprets secret wisdom. It appears that you will be given an opportunity to enter a formal learning environment or group of some kind. You will be part of a group identity and you will grow and better understand yourself as a result. If you are struggling to follow rules then you need to understand that life is a learning process. Sometimes we need to accept that others may be a good source of guidance if we can just listen. At other times we are the ones with the answers. If in doubt consult your inner wisdom. Rules are good sometimes just don't allow them to hold you back.

The Chariot

Your mind can be likened to a chariot being pulled by wild horses. You need to keep careful control of the reigns to gain victory. You will be victorious but only by working with others not against them. You cannot pull the horses in any other direction without their say so. Analyse the problems you keep having to face and look at what behaviour of yours needs to change.

The Lovers

Once in a reading this card came up along with another that showed past love returning. That night my partner did not return home. A few months later I discovered that one of our friends had been a past love of his and that on this particular night he had stayed with her.

The lovers signifies that there are choices to be made regarding love. It can sometimes point to a love triangle and asks the question 'do I want love or lust?' 'security or passion?'. This card can point to infidelity and also to the need to love oneself. Only when you love yourself will your energy attract a love that will be fully rewarding. Follow your heart and if you can, choose love.

Justice

The justice card signifies legal or formal matters. If signifies fairness, truth, doing the right thing. It can indicate Karmic reward for past deeds. Take responsibility for your actions. Reap what you sew and learn lessons. The past will continue to throw little reminders at you until you learn and break the cycle.

The Hermit

The hermit signifies a time for reflection. You need to be alone to look back at the past before you move into the future. Meditate and look within for answers.

Try to take life at a slower pace for a while. Spend some time alone recharging your batteries. Maybe you are seeking spiritual truths or trying to find yourself. The answers are within.

The Wheel of Fortune

The wheel of fortune is a symbol of fate. Of wisdom beyond our own. The wheel of fortune will turn in your favour, you are about to get a helping hand along your path. You will have great insights if you stand back and look at the bigger picture. Fate is about to make an appearance. It will probably hit you like a whirlwind. Who knows what it brings or where it may take you but just try to enjoy the ride.

Strength

Strength is symbolic of inner strength of a happy energy that will give you the courage to face life head on. Be wary of losing control. You have the strength to deal with anything that comes your way but be careful not to become a destructive force. Don't hurt anyone in the process.

The Hanged Man

The hanged man is telling you that the answer is to let go. This is how we win. The hanged man has sacrificed himself but is victorious. He tells us that by standing still we will take great strides.

Take a different perspective. The best answer to a problem is not always the obvious one. When you want something greatly, sacrifice it. When you want to act, don't. Wait. This will bring what you want.

Death

I read the cards for a friend once. He had the death card and the 10 of swords in the reading. A few weeks later I had a strong feeling that something was about to happen. I walked through the town awaiting it and when nothing happened I bought a newspaper. When I opened it I saw that same friend. He was dead. He died a few weeks after his father.

Death can of coarse mean death. Death of the physical. The spirit will always exist. It can also mean the quick, final ending of something in your life. Something is ending and it is likely to be painful. Pain is not to be feared, it is an essential part of our soul's growth. Change can be scary especially when it's so final but it can lead to better things. When one door closes another opens.

Temperance

Temperance is all about balance. About being calm and one with body, mind and spirit. The card hints that we should practice moderation in all things and self restraint. No matter what goes on around you practice being still and keeping balance. The card may be a warning that illness could prevail if balance and moderation are not practiced or it could be a sign that you need to look for an opportunity to bring together opposing parties through compromise. The card generally signifies good health and well being.

The Devil

The devil is warning you to be careful of becoming trapped or being frivolous. You may have more money at your disposal or find yourself in a situation where greed or ego could become a problem. The surrounding cards will tell you more but don't fear the card. You are the one in control.

The Tower

Ooh the tower. Whether or not this card is positive or negative lies with your ability to respond to change. The tower is going to fall. You cannot stop that but you can rebuild the tower and maybe arrive at a better building! Change is inevitable.

The Star

This is a lovely card. A card of hope. Of light in the darkness. A wish will be granted. If somebody has been ill the card can be a sign that they will recover. Make your life a work of art. Surround yourself with beauty and feel grateful for the people and things you have in your life and you will attract abundance.

The Moon

Something is not as it seems. The moon is the card of intuition, of the unconscious and so it foretells secrets. The moon is telling you to beware and above all else trust your inner voice. It will see you through.

The Sun

The sun is a card pointing to renewed energy and vitality and truth. It may point to fertility or the birth of a child and it highlights warmth and peace. This is a good time to make decisions and tests will be successful. If the questioner is pregnant this card can herald the birth of a boy or twins.

Everything in life will suddenly be brighter and things go well.

Judgement

Plans will come to fruition bringing the rewards you have earned. If there is a decision to be made use logic rather than intuition and be prepared to make major decisions. The next chapter of your life is about to begin and if you have planned well it will be a good one.

The World

Life is wonderful. This card is a good omen that highlights success and accomplishment. In order to receive you must give. Be kind, be generous for the world is about to reciprocate.

This points to the completion of something, the successful ending where you can enjoy just sitting back and revelling in your glory for a while.

The Ace of Wands

This card is showing endless possibilities in the areas of creativity, excitement, adventure and courage. You will be enthusiastic about something, maybe a gift or an opportunity. You may have to take a risk though. Choose the path that will push you to your limits and excite you. A new beginning is coming and you will be at your best.

The Ace of Cups

A new relationship is highlighted with this card. It will change something inside of you and you may discover that even though you didn't know you wanted this new relationship or friendship it has stirred feelings inside that you like. This is a good omen for new relationships.

The Ace of Swords

The Ace of Swords is a positive sign that your new idea or plan is a good one. The sword will cut through anything that stands in your way. Stand firm and victorious and move forward!

The Ace of Pentacles

This is a great card for prosperity so if you are considering a new business venture, go for it! It symbolises new opportunities and favours any business dealings or career that is already in place. This is good news for health, wealth and home.

The Two of Wands

The two of wands can signify some kind of power struggle. You need to carefully examine your responsibilities and decide if you wish to lead or to follow. If you decide to lead then be a strong leader. If you choose to follow then do so with grace. There are opportunities available but they come with responsibility and there may be a need to accept the word of authority.

The Two of Cups

This card indicates a good relationship. A balanced relationship or partnership that could progress further. It symbolises cooperation, loyalty, sharing and affection. A true partnership.

The Two of Swords

Do you feel like you are being pulled in two directions? Are you at a cross roads? Neither choice is good or bad, the surrounding cards may give you more information but this card suggests that you need to choose.

The Two of Pentacles

Do you feel like you are struggling to find enough time in the day or enough money to survive? Sit down and work things out and try to find balance. Balance is the key. If money is the issue then maybe you could budget or cut some costs? Maybe you just need to find a balance between the physical and the spiritual?

The Three of Wands

Carry on with your efforts. This number is all about growth. There is a lot more to be done, a lot more you can achieve. The universe is leaving you little signs to light your way so just follow them. Don't rush into anything just yet.

The Three of Cups

Are you having a baby? If not then this card is all about communication. It tells us to get out and spend time with family and friends. Find joy in the people around you. There is lots of love to be shared.

The Three of Swords

I have had this card in the past to signal a breakup of my relationship. It foretells heartache. Pain is either already here or it's on the way. It is a necessary part of life and you will grow from it. It may clear the way for something more positive.

The Three of Pentacles

This card can signify an apprenticeship or a time of learning a new trade. It will be beneficial and you will reap the rewards. It may be some kind of group effort but either way you will reap financial rewards.

The Four of Wands

The four of wands is telling you that something exciting is about to happen! It may be a celebration of some sort or a surprise. It will bring with it feelings of freedom and exhilaration. If you have been feeling trapped in some area of your life then break free! A new happy period is calling.

The Four of Cups

Sometimes we long for love but we fail to see that until we learn to love ourselves, to feel truly grateful for all that we have we risk blocking new opportunities. Are you failing to see what is right in front of you because you are too focused on what's going on inside?

We all need to take time out to look within and if this is what you are doing then that's a positive thing. Just be careful not to take things for granted because nothing in life is guaranteed to last forever. If you are stuck in an emotional rut, meditate, use your time productively to find the way through it.

The Four of Swords

This indicates a time for rest and reflection. Take a break and if you have been ill allow time to heal. You may be facing a big event and need to calm yourself beforehand.

Whatever the situation it's a time for calm and rest and meditation.

The Four of Pentacles

Does somebody want to be in control? Is somebody having a tantrum? Don't let the urge for control get out of hand. It can be dangerous and have a really negative effect on others. People need to feel free and if you are dragging them down with control issues you may lose them. Is it you being controlled? Are you refusing to face up to the fact that change is needed?

Total control is impossible. Sometimes you just have to let things flow.

The Five of Wands

Look, negative energy will only ever attract negativity. Just because you are grumpy it doesn't mean you should spread the grumpiness! You may feel that life is unfair. That everything is irritating you. You may feel that the competition is just too great for you to compete.

Competition is a good thing. It challenges us and challenges help us grow. Just let go of that breath that's stuck in your chest and exhale. Don't fight it.

The Five of Cups

Loss is something that most of us fear. It carries a big black cloud. We don't want let go, to say goodbye to the things or people that we love. Nothing in the physical realm is forever. You probably already know what it is you are about to lose.

Don't despair. Use this warning as a way to prepare yourself. Be ready for it and accept rather than fight. The nature of our sorrow is often that we refuse to let go. Letting go will allow other things and people to come into our lives. Letting go is what we have to do.

The Five of Swords

Do you need to start putting yourself first or are you guilty of being too self absorbed? Are you being used in some way? If you need to break free then do so but try not to hurt too many in the process or you won't feel good about it.

Has a crime been committed? By yourself or someone else? Whatever the problem try to see the bigger picture. You are here to grow as a soul and every experience is a learning opportunity. Find the solution that is best for everyone involved.

The Five of Pentacles

Poor you! Whether the problem is health, work or relationships you are feeling rejected. You are neglecting your health and you need to stop this and take care of yourself.

When money is tight everything seems harder. Fear always looms threatening to make our lives even worse.

Look, there is always comfort near. It is around you and within you but you need to look in the right place. Things are tough but this is just a phase. Things will get better. Big hugs!

The Six of Wands

You have worked hard and success is on the way. Your efforts will be recognised, maybe even publically. Your self esteem will be high but take care not to get a superiority complex! Pride comes before a fall.

Enjoy your success but don't feel the need to put others down to feel good.

The Six of Cups

This card is symbolic of childhood emotions and characteristics. This card represents innocence. If the questioner is concerned about a cheating partner or some other sort of accusation then this card points to innocence.

It's the card of kind deeds, family, celebration and youth.

The Six of Swords

Are you moving or just entering a new phase of life? Are you stuck in a rut or feel like life has lost its meaning? Maybe it's time for a change or to take a little holiday? Things are slowly getting better, take some time right now decide what or where you will go next and if you feel need it's a great time for a holiday.

The Six of Pentacles

Ooh things are changing for the better! Especially when it comes to money. You may get a windfall or some kind of monetary gift but it heralds the start of a positive phase for you.

The Seven of Wands

If there is any sort of competition coming up then you will win. Things will go very well even though you do still have a little self doubt. Do it anyway! If you have been considering setting up a business then go for it!

The Seven of Cups

You may be faced with temptation. Will you risk your status quo and give in to it? Evaluate your choices carefully right now. Often when we are faced with too many options or too many things to do we don't do any of them well. Take some time to calm down and reflect. Maybe you need to let go of some things and focus more on others.

The Seven of Swords

Is someone spying on you? Are you interfering in someone's life where you shouldn't? This card can show that someone is behaving badly. If you suspect someone of cheating you may be right.

The Seven of Pentacles

This is a positive card. You may be seeing some return on investments or work from the past is paying off. You have money and energy to make this a positive phase of life.

The Eight of Wands

Are you looking for commitment that isn't coming?

Things may be a little uncertain right now and you feel fed up with waiting. The card tells you to be patient and wait a little longer. You have done all you can and now you just have to wait.

The Eight of Cups

Do you feel that something may no longer be working? Relationship, job, life? You may need to move on. It will be sad, changes usually are but it may be in your best interests. If your intuition tells you to go then go. Better times lie ahead.

The Eight of Swords

Are you afraid of moving forward? Don't be. You have everything you need right there inside of you. Get to the truth of what it is you really fear. There is nothing to fear but fear itself. If you never fight then ok you will never lose but you will also never win.

Do not fear the unknown. Destiny awaits.

The Eight of Pentacles

This card can herald a new job. There will be hard work but that's a good thing. Just be prepared and don't be afraid to ask for help. The effort you put in is needed. Just have a clear vision of what it is you wish to accomplish and if you are going to work so hard take time to relax too.

The Nine of Wands

Ok. Take a breath and calm down. You are feeling overwhelmed. Look when you sit down and take the time to look beyond the emotions at the heart of the problems they aren't so bad. Make a list with three columns. Column A-problem, Column B-How can I solve it, Column C-How will that make me feel?

Ask for support if you need it.

The Nine of Cups

Your wish is just about to come true! There are good things coming your way, your hopes and dreams are manifesting into reality. You will be lucky, positive, happy, everything will go well although sometimes you may need to be the catalyst.

The Nine of Swords

Take notice of your breathing. Sometimes our posture and poor breathing habits can make us feel anxious. What are you worrying about? If something is worrying you then put steps in place to fix it. Worrying won't help. Take action.

The Nine of Pentacles

Your money worries are coming to end and you will be happy and full of energy. There will be success in whatever your reading is focused on, love, home, career, whatever it is you can't lose.

The Ten of Wands

This card is telling you that you have the strength to carry the weight of the responsibilities you are under. You may be going through a period where your commitment is being tested, you are feeling the pressure. Rest assured though, you have everything you need to get through it.

The Ten of Cups

This card points at a period of fulfilment in the area of love. You truly feel that life is good and you have everything you need. Happiness and success will follow when this card appears. It may mean you create a family or a business or some other type of group effort.

The Ten of Swords

Ooh...the ten of swords warns you that you will have to make a difficult choice. Things won't be easy and you may be betrayed. Keep your wits about you. Maybe now is the time to reflect on the lessons you have learned. Admit defeat. True success doesn't mean there were no mistakes. It means you made many mistakes but have grown from each and every one.

The Ten of Pentacles

This card tells you that you can relax. You have security and should not fear losing anything. All that you have is here to stay. You will be passing on wisdom to the next generation and money may be given to you as an inheritance. Listen to the wisdom of elders and rejoice in family.

The Page of Wands

You may be doubting yourself. This card is telling you that through mistakes you have grown. You are not the same person you were. Trust yourself. Have faith. You are part of the whole. Part of a perfect system of unimaginable proportions and everything you need is inside of you. Believe in yourself, believe in others for you are all part of the divine.

The Page of Cups

This card signifies going back to school or to some kind of learning. You are curious about matters and have a thirst for learning, maybe of a deeper nature. There is sound advice available if you look for it. It appears to be a positive move though. Look at the surrounding cards.

The Page of Swords

Even though you are not aware of it somebody has your back. Someone out there is doing something to help you. This card shows that things will go your way thanks to an unseen force. Your path ahead is smooth so go forward without fear.

The Page of Pentacles

Whoever this card represents is someone that maybe you cannot trust. It could well be yourself but this card points to someone who is easily distracted and always going from one thing to the next without actually finishing anything. If it does represent a partner you probably feel great when you are with them, it's when you are apart the doubt kicks in!

The Knight of Wands

The knight is always looking for adventures and challenges. Always looking for opportunities to save the world, to do good for others. He is calling to you to wake the knight inside of you. Telling you to do something that you can be proud of. You may be on your travels!

The Knight of Cups

Are you considering marriage or some other kind of partnership? Forget the doubts and let the knight carry you off on his horse with passion and excitement and celebration.

The Knight of Swords

Ok so it's time for action. Get off the fence and make your mark in life. This knight is honest and trustworthy and strong in the face of defeat. If he represents someone in your life then you can trust them. Follow your wildest dreams.

The Knight of Pentacles

Take care in matters related to finance. Exercise caution and be sure to read the small print. In order to be successful you must plan carefully and divide your resources with vigilance.

The Queen of Wands

Maybe an old friend will appear or someone is in need of a friend. The queen is loyal and dependable and stands by those she cares for knowing that at times everyone needs emotional support. She is a good listener and offers sound advice.

The Queen of Cups

This card indicates good fortune in affairs of the heart. She loves all things beautiful and artistic and adores her family, appreciating all that life has given her.

The Queen of Swords

You shall have what your heart desires. You have been through very difficult times, times that would break most people yet here you are fighting, surviving and remaining true to yourself. You deserve a great big hug! Stay strong, things will get better.

The Queen of Pentacles

You are a shrewd business person beneath the surface. You are charming and graceful, popular and sociable, and nice, always nice...until you have to be otherwise. You know how to get what you want and by damn you will get it!

The King of Wands

True honesty begins within. Be honest with yourself and with those around you. You may be influenced by a strong, honest man who always keeps to his word. A handy man who may run his own business or is just bossy by nature! This is the kind of person that provides.

The King of Cups

This card shows that if you are looking for love, your mate is on their way and it will last, if you have a love then it is a good one. Your love is musical and artistic and always willing to help.

The King of Swords

You may be facing an ethical dilemma. You will make the right choice eventually. Stand by your beliefs. If you stay true to yourself you will remain on the right path.

The King of Pentacles

The King of Pentacles makes a great husband. He is a provider and will give you all the nice things in life. He struggles to talk about feelings but is very passionate about his work and about providing for his family.

Dreams

Your dreams will be a great guide to understanding what is going on in your subconscious and maybe even what is about to happen in your life. Monitor them and it will allow you to let go of energy that no longer serves you.

Abdomen

To see an abdomen in a dream is a sign that prosperity is on its way. If you have pain in your abdomen it is a sign of good health and good news concerning illness.

Abortion

To dream of an abortion is a sign that you should give something up.

Abroad

To go abroad in a dream is telling you that you will soon be on your travels.

Abundance

To dream that you have lots is a warning to gather and save all you can so that you will be secure.

Abuse

To dream of abusing someone tells you that your financial situation will improve. If you are being abused then illness may follow so take care of your health.

Accident

Whatever the object is that caused the accident should be avoided for a day or day or two. If you dream of a car accident avoid travelling in one.

Acorns

To see an acorn in your dream is a sign that success will follow.

Actor

To see an actor in your dreams is a sign that you have psychic abilities that you may not have been aware of. Do regular energy work to strengthen them and become more aware of them.

Agony

To dream of being in agony is a sign that you have a friend in need.

Album

To look through a photo album in a dream warns of impending accidents.

Almond

To dream of eating almonds tells you of journeys yet to come.

Ambition

To dream of feeling ambitious tells you that you will soon see good fortune in your career.

Amethyst

You may be about to lose someone close to you.

Ancestors

To dream of your ancestors points to a period of good fortune in matters related to communities.

Ancient

To dream of anything ancient is a sign that you will be well respected.

Angels

To see an angel in your dream tells you that someone will be very ill but will recover.

Apple

To see an apple in your dream is a sign of happiness yet to come.

Argument

To dream of an argument is a sign of good luck.

Art

To dream of a art is a sign that you will get a promotion or will rise in your career.

Awake

To dream that you have woken up is a good omen. Happiness is coming your way.

Baby

To see a happy baby is a sign that love is on the way.

Baking

To dream that you are baking is a sign that good fortune is on the way.

Balloon

If you dream of a balloon rising then avoid taking a trip. Balloons can be a sign of loss.

Baptism

To dream of being baptised is a sign that you may be in need of some spiritual time. Some time alone to reflect and reconnect with the universal life force.

Bargain

To dream of finding a bargain is a good sign that something is about to achieve success.

Barking

If you hear a dog barking you should beware of impending danger.

Beach

To dream of the beach is often a sign that you need time alone to reflect on the past and plan the future.

Beauty

To dream of beauty is a good omen and you will be happy.

Bed

To dream of making a bed is a sign that you will find a lover.

Beetles

To dream of beetles suggests money worries. Unless you kill them of coarse!

Bicycle

To dream of riding a bicycle tells you that you have good prospects and bright future.

Birds

Birds are a sign of good fortune and happiness unless they are injured in some way, then they are a sign of poverty and ill health.

Blackberries

To dream of blackberries is a sign that something is need of protection.

Blood

To dream of seeing blood on clothes is a warning to be careful of people you cannot trust, most likely at work. Beware of being betrayed by friends or acquaintances.

Body

To see a lovely body in a dream is a sign that success is coming.

Books

To dream of books is a sign of pleasure and possibly riches.

Box

To open a box is a sign of travels and surprises.

Brother

To dream of your brother is a sign that financial affairs will be promising.

Butter

To dream of eating butter is a sign that good health and prosperity will be yours.

Cactus

To dream of a cactus is a sign of good luck! Something good is about to happen.

Can

To dream of opening a can is a sign that a secret is about to be revealed.

Cancer

Dreaming of illness often means the opposite so to dream of cancer is a sign of recovery from illness.

Car

To dream of a car is a sign that you will keep moving forward in life even though it may not feel that way.

Career

To dream of a career means that something significant or life changing is about to happen.

Carpet

Carpets are a sign of luxury. If you have been through a difficult time things will get better.

Cash

To dream of cash is a sign that prosperous times lay ahead for you.

Castle

To dream of a castle is a sign that a wish will soon be granted.

Childbirth

To dream of childbirth is a sign that it is time to secure financial stability for yourself and family.

Christmas

To dream of Christmas is a good omen telling of financial gains and health.

Classroom

To dream of being in a classroom is a sign that someone from your childhood will return and change your life.

Coconut

Dreaming of a coconut is a sign that you should be on the lookout. You may be about to find something of value.

Cold

If you dream of having a cold take care not to take your bad moods out on others! Especially family and friends.

Cook/Chef

To dream of being a chef is a very good dream indeed. If you dream of serving people it is likely that you will rise into a position of great repute.

Dad

To dream of your father is a sign that you are honourable and will make the right choices.

Daffodil

This dream is telling you to hold on to hope no matter what. You will come through these times reenergised and happy.

Daisy

To dream of a daisy is a sign that a very dear wish will be soon be granted.

Dancing

To dream of dancing is a sign that you will soon be engaged in a very happy love affair.

Daughter

To dream of your daughter is a sign that you will soon be called upon to support someone in need.

Deaf

To dream that you are unable to hear is a good sign that you will deal with your current worries without too much fuss.

Devil

To dream of the devil is a warning that you may be about to get into something that will be difficult to get out of. Maybe some kind of entrapment situation. Think everything through carefully before committing.

Dish

If you dream of a dish you will soon find your soul mate.

Door

Doors are symbolic of opportunities. If the door is closed you may be missing something, if it is open then opportunities await.

Dragon

If you dream of a dragon it is a sign that you are safe and will be blessed with good fortune and happiness.

Drink

To see someone drink in a dream tells of drinking of knowledge from the golden chalice. You may be entering formal education and will be successful in all forms of learning.

Ear

To see ears in a dream is a sign that news is on the way.

Eat

Eating is generally a sign of good fortune to come.

Education

To dream of learning is a sign that you will be successful and happy.

Embarrassment

To dream that you are embarrassed is a sign that you should stop worrying so much about what others think.

Envelope

To seal an envelope in your dream is a sign that you will have a long and happy marriage.

Envy

To dream of feeling envious is a good omen foretelling luck and success.

Eyes

To see eyes in your dream points to a successful project or career that will bring success and professional respect.

Face

To see normal happy faces is a sign of pleasurable pursuits with friends. To see a scary face is not a good omen and you should expect some bad news.

Fairy folk

To dream of fairies may be a sign that you will have a child or it could be the birth of a new project or job.

Falling

To dream of falling suggests failure of some sort. Maybe you are clinging to something that you need to let go of. It is often said that if you hit the ground when you fall it is an omen of death.

Family

To dream of family, if positive, is a sign that you may get the chance to go on holiday soon.

Feet

To see your feet in a dream is a sign that you may be heading in the wrong direction. Stop and think carefully about where you are heading.

Ferns

To walk amongst the ferns suggests that you will soon be taking part in an exciting adventure.

Flight

To dream of flying is a sign that you are trying to accomplish something that is very big and you may feel that it is beyond you. Don't fear it may just be within reach.

Flowers

To dream of flowers is a sign that your luck is good and you should maybe enter competitions or buy a lotto ticket!

Fox

To dream of a fox is a warning that someone may be deceiving you.

Fun

To dream of having fun is a sign of good fortune and happy times.

Funeral

To dream of attending a funeral is an omen of death of some kind. It could be death in the literal sense or the final ending of a chapter.

Future

To dream of the future is a sign that good news is on it's way.

Game

To dream of playing games is a sign that you will be married.

Garbage

To dream of garbage is a sign that you have come from a poverty stricken past but will see a much brighter future.

Garlic

To dream of garlic suggest some kind of award, possibly in competitions.

Gate

To dream of a gate is a sign that opportunities await.

Ginger

To dream of ginger tells of passion ahead.

Glove

To dream of a glove tells of marriage and security.

Gold

To dream of gold is a promise of new beginnings.

Grapes

To dream of grapes is a sign that wealth will be yours and that you have the ability to be of service to others in an inspirational way.

Grass

To dream of grass suggests that life will get a lot easier and there may be some sort of gain.

Gun

To dream of a gun can be a sign of potential danger or it could just be that you are on the defensive about something.

Hair

Hair is often symbolic of your state of mind in a dream.

Half Moon

To dream of the half moon may be a sign that you are about to travel. Beware of things going on behind the scenes and listen to your intuition.

Hands

If the hands are large you may soon achieve a long held goal. If they are rough it may suggest that you need to show your softer side a little more.

Handwriting

To dream of handwriting tells of success in business matters.

Hate

To dream of hate is a sign that someone around you is not happy with themselves and may take this out on you. Don't take it to heart.

Herbs

To dream of herbs is a good omen for a happy marriage and tells of good times ahead.

Hill

To dream of climbing a hill is symbolic of achieving some sort of goal.

Holly

To dream of holly suggests that somebody up there is protecting you. It also heralds a new and positive phase.

Hotel

To dream of a hotel suggests that you will take on more responsibility at work.

Hug

To dream of a hug suggests and long and happy relationship with children is on the cards.

Husband

To dream that you have a husband suggests that you may soon be married.

Hypnotise

To dream that you have been hypnotised suggests that a secret may be uncovered or that you may have to reveal a hidden part of yourself.

Ice cream

Good times, youthfulness, fun and laughter lie ahead.

Idea

To have a great idea in a dream is an omen of extraordinary luck.

Incest

To dream of incest is a warning that you should beware not to get involved in anything immoral.

Inheritance

To dream of this is usually a sign that it is about to happen.

Island

To dream of being on an island denotes a slow but steady rise to success.

Jaguar

To dream of a jaguar is a warning to beware of jealousy and gossip.

Jasmine

To dream of jasmine is a sign that you will fall in love.

Jigsaw

To dream of a jigsaw may mean that some area of your life is about to fall out place.

Joke

To hear a joke in your dream is a sign that an unwelcome visitor is on their way.

Juice

To dream of juice is a sign that help is on it's way.

Key

To see a key in your dream is a sign that you have a skill that may lead to many opportunities.

Kiss

To dream of a kiss signifies betrayal.

Knife

To dream of a knife warns of strife!

Label

To dream of noticing a label is a sign that business ventures will be profitable.

Lake

To see a body of water in your dream is symbolic of your emotional state. If the water is calm and welcoming then all is well but if it is rough then you have worries than need to be faced.

Lamb

This could mean a number of things. Are you being called to sacrifice something in order for something better to develop? Generally though if all is well in the dream it highlights positive change.

Laughter

To dream of laughter is a sign of success and good friends.

Leaf

To dream of a leaf is symbolic of growth in all areas of life.

Lighthouse

To dream of a lighthouse is a sign that help will become available when you most need it.

Lion

To dream of a lion is a sign that someone is seeking your help.

Love

To dream of love denotes happiness, security, peace of mind.

Magic

To dream of magic suggests that your energy field will slowly brighten to attract new and positive changes.

Magnet

To dream of a magnet suggests that you will be irresistible and have a choice of lovers.

Marshmallows

To dream of marshmallows is a sign that you will soon be introduced to someone who makes you feel all mushy inside!

Mermaid

Mermaid dreams are often signs that you are suppressing your femininity. Embrace it! Enjoy it!

Milk

Milk symbolises your maternal instinct and motherly love. It is a sign of good health and happy family.

Moon

If you dream of looking back at the moon you will have good luck. Dreams of the moon are usually a good omen for luck, love and plenty.

Mud

To dream of mud is a sign that someone is gossiping about you.

Murder

To dream of murder is a warning about your own anger. Take care to control it. Anger is a negative emotion and nothing positive can come from it.

Naked

To be naked in a dream highlights your vulnerability. You may be feeling helpless.

Nausea

Is there a situation in your life that is making you ill? There may be a situation in your life that your subconscious is telling you is unhealthy.

Nettle

To dream of nettles is a sign that you may have to be tough. A situation may arise in which you have to stand your ground and be strong.

Nose

If you have a red nose you will have financial success. Are you being a bit nosey?

Notes

To write or read a note in your dream is a sign that a message is on the way.

Oak

Oak points to strength, wealth and wisdom. Taking the time to lay firm foundations and enjoy them.

Occult

To dream of the occult may be a sign that you are feeling a little over sensitive and easily affected by the people around you.

Ocean

Water is symbolic of your emotions but an ocean dream often means that you are feeling powerful and free.

Olives

To see olives in a dream is a sign of healing, hope and peace.

Orchard

To see an orchard is a sign that you will live a happy life of abundance.

Ouija

To dream of the Ouija board is a warning that a secret will be revealed that is likely to cause you shame.

Paint

To dream of paint is a sign that you will be expressing yourself in unique ways. Colours can have significance too. If it you who are painting then success in projects is foretold.

Pyjamas

This dream suggests that you are in need of a little rest. Take some time out and pamper yourself.

Palace

Success will soon be yours and it will bring you a life of abundance.

Panic

To feel panic in a dream is a sign that you are not feeling in control of your destiny. Meditate, take some time to reconnect.

Parcel

To see a parcel in a dream is a sign that you have some skill or talent of which you are currently unaware.

Parsnips

To dream of parsnips is a good omen for business affairs but a negative sign for love. Maybe you can use the money you earn in your career to a little more and find love!

Pen

To dream of a pen is indicative of your creative abilities and suggests that communication will soon be made that will allow you to express those talents.

Pillow

To dream of pillows is a sign that it is time to relax and be comfortable for a little while. Take a bubble bath and watch some light hearted movies in your pyjamas!

Popcorn

To dream of popcorn is a sign that you have a positive outlook on life and your creative genius will bring you riches.

Queen

To dream of a queen symbolises growth, intuition and personal power.

Question

To dream that you are asking a question may be a sign that you are doubting yourself and in need of support or guidance.

Raspberry

To dream of raspberries highlights a very delicate matter that you are currently dealing with.

Road

To dream of a road is a sign of your sense of direction in life. If the road is clear and nice then you will progress smoothly through life.

Ruby

This dream highlights sexual desires and passion. Beware of charming people who only want a casual affair.

Sale

To dream of a sale is a sign that new opportunities await.

Sand

To dream of sand is a sign that your perspective on life is shifting.

Scenery

To dream of enjoying scenery is a sign that life is doing well and you are enjoying what it has to offer.

School

To dream of school may mean that you will get close to old friends. It can also mean that you have learned spiritual lessons which will see you through life.

Shame

To dream of shame is a sign that you may be feeling guilty for past actions.

Storm

To dream of a storm is a sign that you are progressing spiritually.

Sunrise

To dream of a sunrise is a sign of new beginnings, of hope and faith in a brighter future.

Table

To dream of a table is a sign that you will establish financial security.

Teacher

To dream of a teacher suggests that you may be seeking advice, guidance or wisdom in the days to come.

Tooth

To dream of teeth is a sign that you get a windfall.

Superstitions

Acorns

It is said that carrying an acorn will bring you prosperity and health. Keep one in the window sill to keep lightning away!

Ambulance

To see an ambulance can be a sign of bad luck. Hold your nose until you see a brown or a black dog.

Apple

Slice an apple through the centre to reveal the star and eat it in candlelight in front of a mirror to see the face of your soul mate.

Place an apple under your pillow to see the love of your life in a dream.

Baby

To predict the sex of a baby hang a ring on a piece of thread over the pregnant tummy. If the ring moves in a circle it will be a girl, if it moves in a straight line it will be a boy.

Bed

Never put a hat on a bed. It will bring bad luck.

If you start making a quilt be sure to finish it or you will never marry.

Always get out of a bed the same side you got in.

Beds should always be positioned east/west.

Bee

If a bee comes into your home it foretells an unwelcome visitor.

If a swarm of bees are seen on a home it is a sign that the house will catch fire.

Bells

Every time a bell rings an angel gets its wings.

Ringing bells will keep the demons away.

Birds

If a bird flies into your home it's a sign that death is near.

Bread

Never turn a loaf of bread upside down after it has been used.

Whoever eats the last slice of bread has to kiss the cook for luck.

To keep ghosts away place a piece of bread and a little coffee under your home.

Putting a piece of bread inside a baby's cot will ward off disease.

Bridge

Never say goodbye on a bridge. If you do you will never see them again. Bridges are symbolic of the crossing from this world to the next.

Broom

Do not lean a broom against a bed!

Sweeping up after dark will bring a stranger calling.

If someone accidently seeps over your feet you will never be married.

Never take a broom to a new home. Always buy a new one.

To ensure an unwelcome visitor never returns sweep the room out behind them.

Butterfly

If the first butterfly of the year that you see is white it will bring you good luck.

Butterflies only hang around where the energy is positive.

Candle

If wax drips down the side of a candle during a séance it is a sign that someone present will die.

If a candle falls and breaks in two be sure bad luck will come to you.

If a candle flame turns blue death is lurking.

It is considered bad luck to fall asleep with a candle burning.

Always light a candle for a birth and a death to make sure you keep away negative spirits.

If you see a moth flying around a candle flame kill it for good luck.

If a candle flame stands tall, a spirit has come through the wall.

Cat

If you see a black cat walking towards you, walk backwards until it has gone and it will bring you luck.

Keep cats away from babies because they will suck out the soul. When my daughter was a few weeks old I found our kitten had crawled into her cot, curled up and fallen asleep on her face!

A black cat crossing your path in moonlight means death.

If you find a white hair on a black cat it will bring your one true love.

Cheeks

If your cheeks turn red someone is talking about you.

Chimney Sweep

If you see a chimney sweep make a wish.

Circle

Circles will protect you from bad spirits.

Clock

If a clock suddenly chimes after a period of not working there will be a death in the family.

Clover

Clover will protect you from naughty fairies and other creatures of the magical worlds.

A four leaf clover brings good luck.

Coins

If you see a coin only pick it up if it's facing head's. Never pick it up if it's tails.

Cough

To cure a cough take a piece of the ill person's hair. Make a sandwich from it and feed it to a dog saying 'eat, eat well you hound, may you be sick and i be sound'.

Cows

It's bad luck to hit a cow with your hand.

Cows seen lying down are a sign of rain.

Crows

One is bad, two is luck, three is health, four is wealth, five is sickness, six is death.

Dandelion

Blow the dandelion seeds to the wind to make a wish or count the number of blows to tell the time.

Using dandelion root for tea will open the gate to the spirit world.

Dogs

It is good luck to be followed by a strange dog.

If a dog walks between a couple then arguments will follow.

When a dog is staring at nothing intently look between his ears to see a ghost.

A dog that howls just once or three times is telling you that death has fallen nearby.

Door

Always leave through the same door you entered.

Ears

If your left ear is burning someone is speaking well of you. If your right ear is burning they are speaking ill.

Easter

Wear new clothes on Easter for good luck.

It is said that if you don't wear something new at Easter dogs will spit on you and crows will peck your eyes out.

Eyes

If your right eye twitches it will bring good luck, left eye is bad luck and may signal death.

If you see someone who's eyebrows meet in the middle don't trust them.

Fish

If you dream of fish someone is pregnant.

Always throw the first fish you catch back in the water.

Fish will get excited and bite if it's raining.

Never say 'pig' while fishing at sea.

Flowers

Never give red or white flowers to someone in hospital.

Always send flowers in odd numbers.

If you can smell flowers someone is about to die.

If you put a daisy under your pillow it will give you a dream of your true love.

Feet

If the sole of your foot itches you will soon make a journey.

Friday

Accidents are more likely on a Friday.

Never begin a trip or project on a Friday.

If a child is born on a Friday it will be stolen by the fairies.

If you cut your hair on Good Friday you will be without headaches for a year.

Frog

If a frog comes into your house it will bring good luck.

Hair

Pulling out one grey hair will make ten grow in it's place.

Hand

An itchy right hand is a sign you will come into money. An itchy left hande is a sign of paying it.

Horseshoe

Hang a horseshoe above a door to bring good luck. Keep it upside down so that the luck never runs out.

Itch

An itchy nose means you will be kissed by a fool. Rub some wood on it.

Knives

If you are given a knife as a gift from lover the relationship is soon to end.

If you place a knife under the bed you are having a baby in it will ease the pain.

Knives crossed at table will bring arguments.

If you drop a knife a man will call.

Knitting

If you knit a piece of your hair into a garment that you give as a gift it will bind the person to you.

Ladder

Never walk under a ladder.

Ladybird

Never kill a ladybird. Always place it on your hand and blow it away.

Milk

Letting milk boil over is a sign that your worries will get out of control.

Mirror

Breaking a mirror will bring seven years bad luck.

Always cover a mirror during thunder.

If a mirror falls from a wall it may be a sign of death.

Do not show a baby their reflection until they older than one.

Don't look at your reflection over someone's shoulder.

Mistletoe

Keeping mistletoe in the house will ward off illness and protect the home from thunder and lightning.

If someone attempts to kiss you under the mistletoe you cannot refuse.

Onion

Cut an onion into four and place it in each corner of the room to absorb an illness.

If you make a wish while burying onions it will come true.

Opal

Opals should only be worn by those born in October.

Owl

Owls like ghosts so if you see one in old house or building it is haunted.

Hearing the hooting of an owl sometimes means death.

Pencils

Always use the same pen or pencil in an exam as you used when you were revising. You will remember the answers.

Pepper

Spilling pepper will be followed by a disagreement with a friend.

If you are giving a peer to a friend always put it down and allow them to pick it up.

Rainbow

If you walk to the end of the rainbow and dig you will surely find treasure.

Raven

Always be kind to Ravens. They are said to carry the soul of King Arthur.

Robin

Make a wish when you see the first robin of spring.

If a robin flies into your home it brings death.

Rosemary

Rosemary will give you a boost to the brain and keep lovers faithful.

Salt

When you spill salt throw some over the left shoulder into the devils face.

Sprinkle salt across your doorway to keep unwanted visitors away.

Scissors

To drop a pair of scissors is a sign that your love is being unfaithful.

Shoes

Never put new shoes on a table.

Never put new shoes upside down.

Sneezing

Always cover your mouth when you sneeze so that your soul doesn't escape and the devil doesn't enter.

Stars

Make a wish on a shooting star.

Swan

If you sew a swan's feather into your lovers pillow they will forever be faithful.

Thirteen

If thirteen people are at a dinner party one will die before the year is through.

Umbrella

Dropping one in the home is a sign that someone is soon to be murdered.

Veil

A veil protects the bride from evil spirits.

Printed in Great
Britain
by Amazon